YOU AND YOUR MILITARY HERO

Building Positive Thinking Skills During Your Hero's Deployment

Fun Activities & Games Included

Sara Jensen-Fritz, MS, Psy.S., Paula Jones-Johnson, BSW, M.Ed., and Thea L. Zitzow, M.Ed.

UFLIPP

ISBN 10: 1-59298-268-9
ISBN 13: 978-1-59298-268-4

Library of Congress Catalog Number: 2008944257
Printed in the United States of America
Eighth Printing: 2013
16 15 14 13   8 9 10

Cover and interior design by Ryan Scheife, Mayfly Design

BEAVER'S POND
PRESS

Beaver's Pond Press, Inc.
7108 Ohms Lane
Edina, MN 55439-2129
(952) 829-8818
www.BeaversPondPress.com

To order, visit www.BookHouseFulfillment.com
or call (800) 901-3480. Reseller discounts available.

TABLE OF CONTENTS

TABLE OF CONTENTS

"We wish this book would have been available for our four children when their Dad was serving in Iraq. Our children had so many mixed emotions and had difficulty expressing them. *You and Your Military Hero* is an excellent resource for anyone who has a "STAR Hero" deployed.

—Sgt. Denver and Mrs. Kelly Heid

TO THE CHILD

Things to Know

This book will become the story about you and your military Hero.

It has many activities for you to do while your military Hero is away. You will learn new ways to:

- Understand your feelings
- Relax
- Think good thoughts

You will draw pictures and share your feelings. This will help you feel good while your military Hero is away.

This is how you use this book:

1. Find an adult you'd like to share your thoughts with while you do the activities in this book.
2. Each week set aside a special time with this adult to work in your book.
3. Follow the book's weekly activities in order.
4. Complete all the activities presented for one week, then, wait a week before moving on to the next group of activities. (Waiting a week gives you time to think about and practice the things you learned.)

FOR THE ADULT

Things to Know

Many times, adults ask children to take a "fix the problem" or "focus on hardship" perspective in order to find solutions to difficult problems and circumstances. The authors feel that children benefit more from approaching difficult times positively. Children need to nourish and encourage their sources of inner joy; from a positive place, they can be more effective in improving their life experiences. *You and Your Military Hero* is intended to assist children during the difficult days of transition of their loved one's military deployment.

This book is unique in four different ways:

1. It is a keepsake in which the child can preserve memories that he or she has illustrated or written about during his or her military Hero's deployment.
2. It contains pages of activities and discussion topics meant to help the child foster positive thinking and to provide the child with the ability to tap into feelings of happiness, even during difficult times.
3. It is a place for the child to document positive coping skills he or she developed during the deployment of a loved one.
4. It contains a systemized way for the child to keep track of his or her feelings each week.

Important:

This book is most effective when children have time to process information and practice skills from each activity session. The authors recommend spending at least thirty minutes with the child on a weekly basis to work on the activities in order as presented for that week. It is also suggested that you re-visit the activities once they are first completed and/or practice learned skills throughout the week.

Disclaimer

This book is not intended to be a replacement for therapeutic treatment by a licensed mental health professional. Adults assisting a child with this book are encouraged to consult a licensed mental health professional if the child exhibits significant signs of stress. Signs of stress may include, but are not limited to, anxiety; depressed mood and/or dark or depressed drawings or writings; sleep disturbances; changes in eating patterns; persistent, uncontrollable anger; and any other behaviors or symptoms that are of concern.

Meet Flipp

"Hi, kids! I'm Flipp. Like you, I have someone I love who is away from home, doing a job in the military. My military Hero was deployed last year. I really miss playing fetch with him. No one else can throw the ball like he does. Since he's been away, I've had extra time on my paws. I've thought up some super fun activities so that you can celebrate you and your military Hero. So let's get started! We'll draw, play some games, and learn how to feel good while your military Hero is away.

I'm here to help and guide you!

This book is illustrated by:

Hollis
_____
(your name)

Age: ____ 6 ____   Grade: ____ K ____

Date I Started This Book: ____ FeB 320 ____
2017

Me and My Family

I'd like to meet your family. On the lines below write about the ways that your military Hero is special to your family.

_____

_____

_____

_____

_____

On the following page, draw a picture of you and your family. Don't forget to include your military Hero.

Me and My Family

How Am I Feeling Today?

Today we're going to learn about feelings. I'm sure you know that there are many different kinds of feelings. You can feel happy or you can feel sad. You can feel scared or you can feel excited. But did you know that there are many *levels* of feelings? Well, there are. We can feel really great, or we can feel pretty bad. You're going to use the ladder on the next page to show how you're feeling for the day. But first you need to figure out how you are feeling. Let's use some stars to show the level of our feelings.

ONE ★ means you're feeling pretty bad. Maybe you are especially missing your special hero today, or maybe someone teased you or everything has gone wrong all day.

TWO ★★ mean you're not feeling okay. Having a two-star day is not as bad as having a one-star, down-and-out day, but a two-star day is still not a good day. Maybe you forgot to bring your homework to school, or maybe it's raining and you can't go to the park after all.

THREE ★★★ mean you're feeling okay. Nothing is out of the ordinary, and nothing has gone wrong. It's a regular day and all is fine. There's no reason to feel bad, but no reason to feel especially great either.

FOUR ★★★★ mean you're feeling pretty good. Maybe you got to play your favorite game at recess, maybe a friend is coming over to your house for a sleep-over, or maybe you got a compliment that made you feel proud of yourself.

FIVE ★★★★★ mean you're feeling great! Maybe you got a super grade on a project that you worked hard on for school. Maybe Mom or Dad took you fishing, or maybe your dog climbed onto your lap and licked your face and made you laugh.

Whenever you see the ladder at the top of a page in this book, I want you to circle the number of stars that show how you are feeling for the day. On page 54 there is a Feelings Check-in Graph. Be sure to place a mark (X) on the graph each time you use the ladder. When you finish this book, you will be able to see how your feelings change over time.

In the box on the next page, draw a picture of how you're feeling today.

Let's Play!

Now let's play a game. Cut out the feeling words found on page 55. Read the feeling word (or have someone read it to you) and figure out on which level of the ladder the feeling belongs. Point to where you think it belongs on the ladder. It's okay if someone helps you!

Where Am I On the Ladder?

Everyone Has Feelings. All Feelings Are Okay.

This is how I am feeling today.

★★★★★ Great!

★★★★ Pretty Good!

★★★ Okay.

★★ Not So Good.

★ Pretty Bad.

There are many different levels of feelings. We will use the stars to gauge our level of feelings each time we meet.

Someone To Always Remember (STAR)

Since this book is all about your military Hero being away, I thought it would be fun to give your hero a special name. From now on we will call your special hero your STAR Hero. This stands for <u>S</u>omeone <u>T</u>o <u>A</u>lways <u>R</u>emember. The star is special to our military Heroes, too, because there are fifty stars on our flag to represent the fifty states in the United States.

Look at the STAR on the next page. See the beams coming out of the STAR? Those beams stand for all the positive feelings you have such as joy, confidence, and all of your good work and your inner strength.

I am proud and grateful to have a military Hero who serves our country and protects our freedom. STAR Heroes are very brave people. I honor your STAR Hero, too. Write your STAR Hero's name on the line provided.

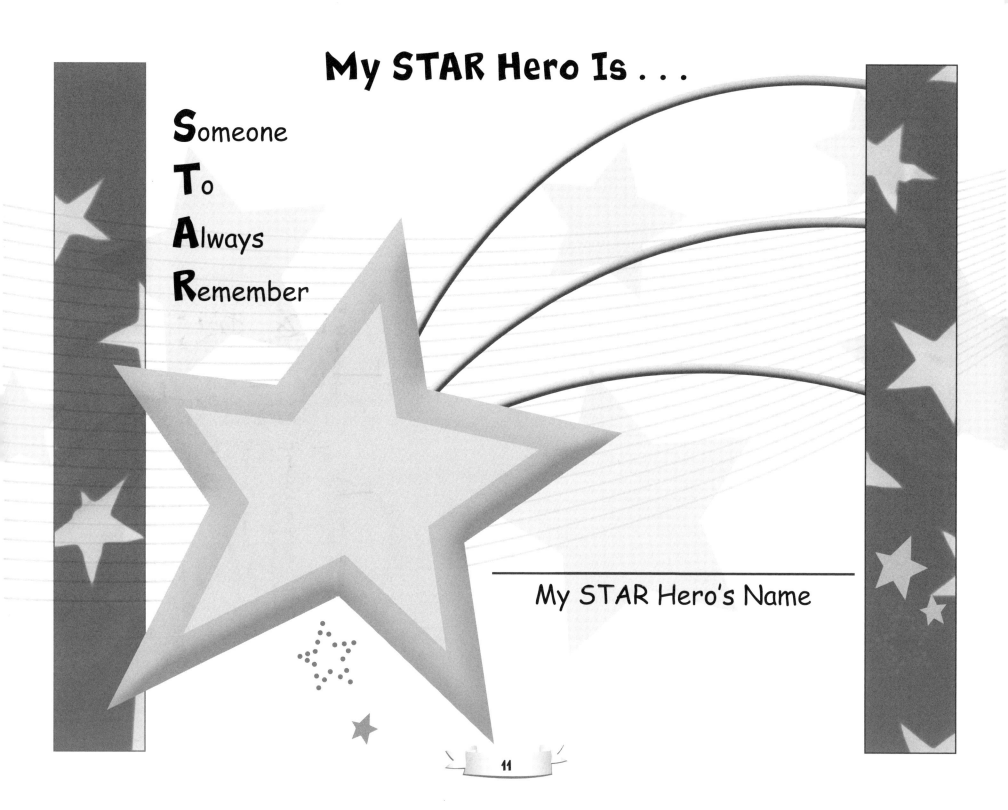

My STAR Hero Is . . .

Someone
To
Always
Remember

My STAR Hero's Name

About My STAR Hero

See the star on the next page? Place a photograph of your STAR Hero in the middle of the star. If you don't have an actual photo of your STAR Hero, you can draw a picture.

Now, think of ways to describe your STAR Hero. Maybe your STAR Hero is funny, can run fast, or likes to cook. On the lines below, write your description of your STAR Hero. I'm sure you know lots of things about your STAR Hero!

_____

_____

_____

_____

_____

_____

This Is My STAR Hero

(Draw or paste picture below)

What Are the Stages of Deployment?

Did you know that there are many branches of military service? Is your STAR Hero in the Army, National Guard, Navy, Marines, Air Force, Air Guard, or Coast Guard?

When STAR Heroes go away to do their military service, we call that "deployment." There are three stages of deployment. Below are descriptions of these three stages.

PRE-DEPLOYMENT is the time when your STAR Hero is about to go to another place in the country or world, but hasn't left yet. You may feel sad or confused as your STAR Hero gets ready to leave.

DEPLOYMENT is when your STAR Hero is on active duty away from home. This is a time when family members have new roles and responsibilities at home because their STAR Hero is not able to be home to help. During this time, there are many ways to keep in touch with your STAR Hero. You can send e-mail messages or write letters.

POST-DEPLOYMENT is when your STAR Hero is home! It's exciting to have your STAR Hero home again, but it also means everyone's roles and responsibilities change again. If your STAR Hero has just arrived home, your family can contact special local, state, or national groups who work with families with military heroes like yours. These special groups can help you understand all the changes that happen when STAR Heroes come home!

On the next page, write the name of the military branch your STAR Hero is serving with. Circle the stage of deployment your STAR Hero is in.

Remember:

- Choose your level for today on the Feelings Ladder and circle it on the next page.
- Record your level for today with an X on the Feelings Check-In Graph (appendix).

My STAR Hero is in the

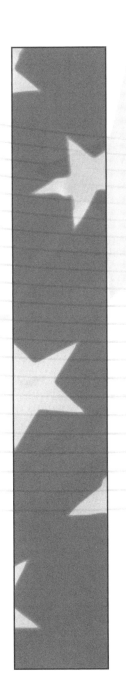

_____

(military branch)

1. Pre-Deployment—still at home, but will be leaving soon

2. Deployment—away from home

3. Post-Deployment—back home

Where Is My STAR Hero?

Where in the world is your Star Hero? Look at a world map, atlas, or globe to find where your STAR Hero is stationed. On the next page, place a star where your STAR Hero is stationed. What do you know about that place? What is the weather like? What games do the children play? With the help of an adult, go to the library or do a search on the Internet and find two facts about this place. Write the facts in the space provided.

Fact: _____

_____

_____

Fact: _____

_____

_____

PART 3

How Have Things Changed For My Family?

Remember when I mentioned that during the deployment stage there would be changes in your responsibilities? The next page lists some of the changes that may happen. Check the ones that have changed for you. Remember that some things in your family will stay the same, but some things will be different.

Change happens to all of us. You change by growing a little bit taller each day, and that's a good thing! You also change by learning new things every day. That's another good thing! What do you think can be a positive or good change during deployment? Maybe you become more responsible and proud of yourself by learning new things like doing the laundry or making your own lunch.

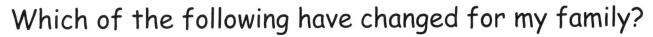

Changing Roles

Which of the following have changed for my family?

_____ who tucks me into bed at night

_____ who gets me up in the morning

_____ who makes dinner, lunch, breakfast

_____ who takes care of my pet(s)

_____ who helps with homework

_____ who reads to me

_____ who does the laundry

_____ who helps me celebrate my birthday

_____ who takes care of me when I'm sick

_____ who makes me an after-school snack

_____ who shovels or plows snow

_____ who does the dishes

_____ who mows the lawn

_____ who takes me places

_____ who takes out the garbage

_____ who gets me to and from school

_____ who says prayers with me

_____ who helps me celebrate holidays

_____ other _____

When my STAR Hero is away, some things are the same
and some things are different.

Staying In Touch
With My STAR Hero

Today I want to give you some ideas about how to stay in touch with your STAR Hero. Look at the next page and read over the suggestions. Choose at least one of them to do each week to stay in touch with your STAR Hero.

In the back of this book is a blank calendar page. Each month, have an adult make a copy, write that month's name at the top of the page, and fill in the dates for each day. Then, every day write down the things that happened in your life that you want to remember. For example, if you scored six points in a basketball game on February 5th, make a note of this in the space for February 5th. You can save these calendar pages to share with your STAR Hero when your STAR Hero comes home, or you can mail a page to your STAR Hero at the end of each month. This way, your STAR Hero will know about what you have been doing!

You might want to save other things, like a special drawing or a school paper or an award, to share with your STAR Hero. Save these things in an envelope and keep it with this book. The envelope is a great place to store the game pieces, too.

Remember:

- Choose your level for today on the Feelings Ladder and circle it on the next page.
- Record your level for today with an X on the Feelings Check-In Graph (appendix).

Staying in Touch With My STAR Hero

I will pick one of the following items to do weekly.

★ email my STAR Hero _____ STAR Hero's email

★ write a letter to my STAR Hero   ★ make a video/DVD to send to my STAR Hero

★ draw a picture and mail it to my STAR Hero   ★ mail a photo of me to my STAR Hero

★ send a care package to my STAR Hero   ★ make a craft to send to my STAR Hero

★ ask my classmates to send letters to my STAR Hero

★ write on my calendar page and send it to my STAR Hero each month

★ go to a special place that helps me think about my STAR Hero

★ write my thoughts and/or feelings in my journal and send it to my STAR Hero

★ create a photo album or collage of my school or home activities to send to my STAR Hero

★ other _____

What Am I Feeling?

Look at the picture of me on the next page. The way my face looks shows you how I am feeling.

Choose three of these feelings from the following page. Draw or write about them below. For example, you could write, "I felt excited when I was invited to a birthday party." Or you could just write, "Birthdays—exciting."

On the next page, color each of the pictures with a color that you think matches the feeling. For example, you might color my angry face red or my happy face yellow.

DRAW   **WRITE**

Flipp's Feelings

Worried

Sad

Stressed

Angry

Surprised!!!

Guilty

Excited!

Happy

Scared

Choosing My Thoughts and Feelings

Sometimes my feelings get heavy and they weigh me down. When I'm sad, like when I miss my STAR Hero, or when I'm mad about something my friend said, my whole body feels weird. Sometimes my body feels tight or tired. This doesn't feel good.

The good news is that I can change how I feel. The best way to change heavy feelings, like feeling mad or sad or scared, is to stop "holding on" to them. We hold on to feelings when we think about them over and over. You can choose not to think about bad feelings over and over again. By practicing the activities in this book or by talking to an adult you trust, you will learn how to let go of the heavy feelings.

Look at my face on the next page. Hanging on to heavy feelings takes work. It's like holding a bag filled with heavy rocks; pretty soon you get tired. If I can let go of my heavy feelings by thinking about something that makes me feel good, I can feel better! It's like putting down that bag of rocks and feeling better . . . lighter. It's easy to lighten up and feel better; it just takes practice!

On the next page, did you notice that I had to actively *choose* to put down the heavy things in order to lighten up? Remember: we can choose how we feel even though we cannot always choose the situation we are in.

Remember:

- Choose your level for today on the Feelings Ladder and circle it on the next page.
- Record your level for today with an X on the Feelings Check-In Graph (appendix).
- Choose one thing to do to stay in touch with your STAR Hero this week.

- Write it here_____

Sometimes My Feelings Get Heavy

Date: ___/___/___

Sad

Angry

But I Know How to Lighten Up

Joyful

Calm

25

My STAR Hero's Wish for Me

I like to feel good. I like to feel happy. My STAR Hero likes to feel happy, too. One way my STAR Hero feels good is by knowing that I am happy. Remember: you can feel good by just being a kid! Go play, be with friends, laugh, run, and jump. Do what makes you happy!

Draw or color a picture of what you like to do and what makes you happy! This is what your STAR Hero wishes for you!

My STAR Hero's Wish for Me

How Can I Feel Good?

Talking to Someone I Trust

When I miss my STAR Hero, I can share my heavy feelings with someone I trust. Talking to someone I trust makes me feel good. Usually that person has a way of looking at things in a positive way. Hanging around positive people can also make me feel good. I know that people are positive when they:

- Make healthy choices for themselves and encourage me to make healthy choices , too.
- Say kind things to me.
- Respect my personal space.
- Listen to me.
- Smile and laugh.
- Accept me for who I am.
- Believe in me.
- Show support for me in many ways.

Draw a picture or write the names of the special people you trust on the next page.

Remember:

- Choose your level for today on the Feelings Ladder and circle it on the next page.
- Record your level for today with an X on the Feelings Check-In Graph (appendix).
- Choose one thing to do to stay in touch with your STAR Hero this week.

- Write it here_____

What Can I Do to Feel Good?

Date: ___ / ___ / ___

I Can Talk to Someone I Trust

Here are some people I can talk to.

(Draw pictures or write names.)

How Can I Feel Good?

Finding Comfort in the Moon

Did you know that everyone, no matter where they are in the world, can see the moon? They just see it at different times, from different places. Sometimes when I miss my STAR Hero, I look at the moon and imagine my Star Hero doing the same thing. I can use my imagination when I want to feel close to my STAR Hero, and you can, too.

Draw a picture of both you and your STAR Hero looking at the moon from different places.

What Can I Do to Feel Good?

I Can Find Comfort in the Moon

This is me, the moon, and my STAR Hero

How Can I Feel Good?

Breathing Deeply

Did you know that when you feel stress you may notice changes in your body? For example, your heart may speed up, you may breathe faster, your muscles may tense up, and it may be hard to think clearly. When you feel stress, you may feel that things are out of control.

When I get excited, nervous, or just plain stressed out, one of the first things I do is take some deep breaths. It helps me calm down. This is how you do it. Sit or lay comfortably. Breathe in. When you breathe in, your stomach rises. That's because it's filling with air. Now breathe out. When you breathe out, your stomach goes back down. Follow the steps on the next page. Try to practice this each night before you go to sleep. The next time you feel stressed, you will know how to breathe deeply. This special breathing will help you feel calm again.

Remember:

- Choose your level for today on the Feelings Ladder and circle it on the next page.
- Record your level for today with an X on the Feelings Check-In Graph (appendix).
- Choose one thing to do to stay in touch with your STAR Hero this week.

- Write it here_____

What Can I Do to Feel Good?

I Can Take 3 Deep Breaths. This Is How I Breathe to Relax.

1. Sit or lay comfortably.

2. Close my eyes.

3. Place my hand on my stomach.

4. Breathe in deeply through my nose. Breathe in 2-3-4.

5. Breathe out softly through my mouth. Breathe out 2-3-4.

6. Do in/out breathing 3 times.

7. My body feels much more relaxed.

Practice each day and remember:
Breathe in 2-3-4. Breathe out 2-3-4.

How Can I Feel Good?

Learning to Relax

A second thing I do that helps me calm down is to tighten and relax my muscles from my toes to my nose. First, I sit or lay comfortably. Then I begin an exercise that's called muscle relaxation. Try it with me! Follow the steps on the next page. I breathe in, hold my breath, and tighten certain muscles. I keep my muscles tight and count to five. Then I breathe out and relax my muscles. Pick one day a week to practice this. I like to do this on Saturday mornings.

- -

Ask an adult to read these eleven steps to you while you practice relaxing.

What Can I Do to Feel Good?
I Can Relax My Body

First I need to lie down or sit comfortably.
Then I need to slow my breathing.

I will breathe in as I tighten my muscles and breathe out as I relax.

1. Tighten my toes and feet. Hold it . . . hold it . . . hold it . . . now relax.

2. Tighten my calf muscles. Hold it . . . hold it . . . hold it . . . now relax.

3. Tighten my thigh muscles. Hold it . . . hold it . . . hold it . . . now relax.

4. Tighten my tummy muscles. Hold it . . . hold it . . . hold it . . . now relax.

5. Tighten my chest muscles. Hold it . . . hold it . . . hold it . . . now relax.

6. Tighten my fingers and hands. Hold it . . . hold it . . . hold it . . . now relax.

7. Tighten my arms. Hold it . . . hold it . . . hold it . . . now relax.

8. Tighten my shoulders. Hold it . . . hold it . . . hold it . . . now relax.

9. Tighten my neck. Hold It . . . hold it . . . hold it . . . now relax.

10. Tighten my face. Hold it . . . hold it . . . hold it . . . now relax.

11. Tighten my whole body. Hold it . . . hold it . . . hold it . . . now relax.

How Can I Feel Good?

Imagining a Calm Place

I can also feel calm when I close my eyes and see or think about my favorite quiet place. Here's a way to practice. Close your eyes and think about what an apple looks like. What color is it? How big is it? Is it the size of your fist, or is it bigger? Now imagine holding the apple and taking a bite. How does it taste? Is it juicy or sour or sweet? You just used your imagination to see and taste the apple.

Now, we're going to do the same thing, only you are going to imagine your very own quiet place. Imagine the details of your quiet place in your mind. I like to picture myself on the beach feeling the warm sun on my fur and the sand under my paws. What about you? Where is your quiet place? Where do you want to go? What do you like to do there? Are you walking in the woods? Are you in a field flying a kite? Are you in your bedroom curled up with your pet? Are you on a playground playing with your STAR Hero?

Imagine your quiet place, and then draw a picture of it on the next page.

Remember:

- Choose your level for today on the Feelings Ladder and circle it on the next page.
- Record your level for today with an X on the Feelings Check-In Graph (appendix).
- Choose one thing to do to stay in touch with your STAR Hero this week.

- Write it here_____

What Can I Do to Feel Good?

I Can Imagine a Calm Place

This is my calm place.

I Have Choices

Do you know what a choice is? You have a choice when you are not forced to do something or when you have more than one thing to pick from. If someone offers you a piece of pie, you can choose to take it or choose not to take it. If someone asks if you'd like a piece of cherry pie or a piece of apple pie, you have a choice! Sometimes we get to make choices, and sometimes others make choices for us. For example, my family chooses when I eat and when we will go for a walk. But I get to choose whether or not to chase a squirrel or to chew on one of my toys.

At the top of the next page, you can see examples of things you can choose and things you cannot choose.

Circle the choices that make you feel the best.

Making certain choices, like having certain feelings, can be positive or negative.

Making positive choices makes you feel proud, which is a positive feeling! Positive choices are good for you. For example, eating an apple can be a positive choice because eating apples is good for us. You should feel proud when you make this choice!

- -

Making negative choices can sometimes feel good, but are not good for us. For example, it may feel good to eat a big bag of candy at first, but too much sugar is not good for our bodies and will make us feel sick. This is why choosing to eat a whole bag of candy is a negative choice.

Remember:

- Choose your level for today on the Feelings Ladder and circle it on the next page.
- Record your level for today with an X on the Feelings Check-In Graph (appendix).
- Choose one thing to do to stay in touch with your STAR Hero this week.

- Write it here_____

I Have Many Choices

I Can Choose

- what to do for fun
- my friends
- what to read
- to tell the truth
- to stay in touch with my STAR Hero

I Cannot Choose

- whether I go to school
- what I look like
- when my STAR Hero is home
- where I live
- my family members

Having Choices Feels Good. How about our thoughts? Do we have choices about how we think?

I Feel Good When I Choose To:

- talk to someone I trust
- relax my body
- watch a funny movie
- exercise
- write to my STAR Hero
- ride a horse
- play with my pet
- go outside to play
- create art
- go for a walk
- read a book
- draw a picture to send to my STAR Hero

- use deep breathing
- imagine a calm place
- play with my friends
- listen to music
- ride a bike
- go to the beach
- go sledding
- make a fort
- build something
- call a friend
- dance

Feeling Good with Flipp Game

The Feeling Good With Flipp game is found on page 57. Cut apart the game cards found on pages 59 and 61.

DIRECTIONS:
Choose one marker or a small object as the game piece. This is a cooperative game: all the players play as a team and use one game piece. The object of the game is to move the marker to Fun Island by making good choices. Take turns drawing cards and reading them aloud. Decide whether the card describes a positive or negative choice, and then move according to the direction. Continue playing until you meet Flipp on Fun Island. If you like, find a fun, energetic song to play at the end of the game and dance! Have fun!

PART 4

I Can Choose My Thoughts

Our brains are always thinking. We think about people, places, and things. Did you know that you have the power to choose what you think about? Did you know that you also have the power to choose *how* you think about something? Remember, we can choose positive thoughts, which are good, or negative thoughts, which are not good. For example, we can choose to think about how terrible it is that our STAR Hero is away. This is a negative thought that can make us feel bad. Or we can choose to think how proud we are of our STAR Hero. This is a positive thought that can make us feel great!

Believe it or not, a good time to practice our positive thinking is during tough times. The next time you have a one-star or a two-star day, try to see if you can feel better and make it a three-, four-, or five-star day. You can do this by changing the way you think about what happened. Replace a negative thought with a positive thought. It's not always easy to do, but you can do it! Find an adult you trust who can help you practice.

We can choose to have a positive or negative thought about the exact same situation. Look at the thought bubbles on the next page. Read each bubble. Each one describes a different situation. Pick one bubble. Imagine that you feel *happy* about what the bubble describes. What happy thought would go with that feeling? Now imagine that you feel *bad* about what the bubble describes. What bad thought would go with that feeling? Do this for each bubble.

Here's an example:

"I got a present that I didn't like . . . "

I imagine that I feel *happy* about this. My happy and positive thought might be: "Wow, she must really like me! It was so kind of her to buy me something."

I imagine that I feel *bad* about this. My bad and negative thought might be: "I hate this present. She never gives me what I want!"

Remember:

- Choose your level for today on the Feelings Ladder and circle it on the next page.
- Record your level for today with an X on the Feelings Check-In Graph (appendix).
- Choose one thing to do to stay in touch with your STAR Hero this week.

- Write it here_____

_____

My friend didn't call me back...

My STAR Hero is deployed...

I got to go to the movies...

I CAN Choose My Thoughts!

I found five dollars on the sidewalk...

I took 2nd place in a race...

I got a present that I didn't like...

My team won the game...

My mom or dad wouldn't buy me something I wanted...

I Can Choose Positive Thoughts

Many of my thoughts are valuable: they are keepers and need to be saved. Thoughts like "I am good at playing ball" and "I am proud of my STAR Hero" are thoughts that are keepers. Sometimes my thoughts are not very good and need to be thrown away. Thoughts like, "I can't read well" or "I'm not good at climbing trees" or "My STAR Hero doesn't miss me" should go into the trash. These thoughts do not make us feel good, and we don't want to keep them.

I have a game called Thought Bank Bingo. My game will help you practice choosing and keeping only those thoughts that help you to feel good.

'THOUGHT BANK BINGO' GAME.
The Thought Bank Bingo game board is found on page 63. Cut apart the game cards found on page 65.

This game may be played alone or as a cooperative game with others. The object of the game is to get a bingo; 5 squares in a row in any direction.

DIRECTIONS:
Put the cards in a cup or bowl. Take one card from the cup and think about how the thought on the card makes you feel. Decide whether that thought is a positive and helpful one, or a negative and unhelpful one. If it is a positive thought, put it in the bank by placing it on top of the picture of a bank on the game board. If it is a negative one, put it in the trash by placing it on the picture of a trashcan on the game board. If you are playing with someone else, let the next person take a turn picking out a card, and deciding if the thought is positive or negative. Continue until you get a bingo.

HAVE FUN!

Remember:

- Choose your level for today on the Feelings Ladder and circle it on the next page.
- Record your level for today with an X on the Feelings Check-In Graph (appendix).
- Choose one thing to do to stay in touch with your STAR Hero this week.

- Write it here_____

_____

I Can Choose Positive Thoughts

I have a choice about what goes into my thought bank!

Positive Thoughts Are Valuable!

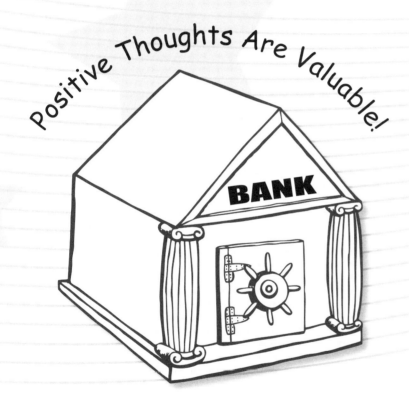

I can choose to keep the thoughts that make me feel good.

Negative Thoughts Are Trash!

I can choose to throw away the thoughts that don't make me feel good.

My Positive Thoughts Lead to Positive Feelings

Did you know that our thoughts and feelings like to hang out together? Remember: there are two kinds of thoughts, positive and negative. Positive thoughts, or thoughts that make you feel good, may make you smile, laugh, or relax. Negative thoughts, or thoughts that make you feel bad, may make you feel mad, sad, or tense.

We can check what kind of thoughts we are thinking by tuning in to how we are feeling. If I feel bad, I can ask myself, "What am I thinking?" Once I know my thoughts, I can decide to keep them or throw them away. Then, just like magic, my feelings change! You can do this, too! Changing our thoughts takes time and practice, though. You have to pay attention to your thoughts and how they make you feel.

Can you think of a time when your thoughts made you feel happy? How about a time when your thoughts made you feel sad? What were you thinking that made you feel happy or sad? In the boxes below, show what you are thinking and feeling right now. In the first box, draw a picture of what you are thinking. In the second box, write about how your thought makes you feel.

Here's an example: "I am thinking about playing fetch with my STAR Hero and I am feeling happy."

HERE'S WHAT I AM THINKING

HERE'S WHAT I AM FEELING

Remember:

- Choose your level for today on the Feelings Ladder and circle it on the next page.
- Record your level for today with an X on the Feelings Check-In Graph (appendix).
- Choose one thing to do to stay in touch with your STAR Hero this week.

- Write it here_____

_____

Positive Thoughts Lead to Positive Feelings

Positive Thoughts hang out with Positive Feelings

They are like best friends.

Stay Positive!

But Remember . . .

If you choose negative thoughts, those thoughts will hang out with negative feelings, and that doesn't feel good.

My Positive Feelings Are Magnets for Good Things

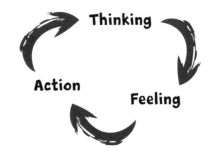

When we choose positive thoughts, we feel good. Did you know that when we feel good, we often choose to do positive things that match that feeling? And did you know that those positive actions will then bring good things into our lives? Well, they will! When you think a positive thought and do a positive action, you are like a big magnet that attracts other positive things into your life.

For example, "I can learn to play catch" is a positive thought. That positive thought will cause me to have a positive feeling, like feeling confident that I can learn to play catch. When I feel confident that I can learn to play catch, I'll choose to practice playing catch even more. Practicing a lot will help me become a better catcher, which will give me even more confidence. The same can happen for you! When you think positively, feel positively, and act positively, you will feel even greater.

On the following page there are three boxes. In the first box, draw or describe one of your goals. A goal might be that you want to go to summer camp, or *be* a better baseball player, or maybe you want to *have* a new bike.

In the middle box, draw or describe one positive thought that will help you reach your goal. For example, if your goal is to have a new bike, a positive thought might be, "I can find ways to earn money."

In the last box, draw or describe at least one thing you need to *do* to reach your goal. For example, to earn extra money for my new bike, "I will have a lemonade stand."

Remember:

- Choose your level for today on the Feelings Ladder and circle it on the next page.
- Record your level for today with an X on the Feelings Check-In Graph (appendix).
- Choose one thing to do to stay in touch with your STAR Hero this week.

- Write it here_____

_____

Positive Feelings Lead To Good Things

When we feel good we attract good things.

Feeling good is like having a very powerful magnet that brings good things to you.

What are some of the good things (or situations) you want in YOUR life? Draw them above.

The Power of My Thoughts

On the next page are four ways to practice keeping your thoughts positive.

First, start each day with a positive thought.
I tell myself, "I'm a good dog." You can tell yourself anything that makes you feel good.

Here are a few of my favorites:
"I'm special. There is nobody else like me."
"Today is going to be a great day."
"My STAR Hero thinks about me every day."
"I can run fast."

In the first blank, write your *own* special positive thought or reminder. Choose a thought that makes you feel good.

Second, pay attention to the thoughts in your 'thought bank.' Keep the good thoughts like "I did great on my spelling test" or "I had fun playing with my friends." Remember, negative thoughts will only make you feel bad. Let those thoughts go. Throw them away! With practice, you will get better at keeping positive thoughts and throwing away negative ones.

Remember:

- Choose your level for today on the Feelings Ladder and circle it on the next page.
- Record your level for today with an X on the Feelings Check-In Graph (appendix).
- Choose one thing to do to stay in touch with your STAR Hero this week.

- Write it here_____

_____

Third, keep positive images in your head throughout the day. Examples of positive images are images of doing something fun with your STAR Hero, getting a hug, or playing a favorite game with a friend. Write *your* favorite image on the following page and use this image when you are *not* feeling good.

Fourth, end each day with a positive thought at bedtime. Close your eyes and think about your STAR Hero. I like to imagine or dream about napping by my STAR Hero's feet. What would you like to imagine or dream about? Write your favorite dream or image of your STAR Hero on the next page. Sweet dreams!

YOUR THOUGHTS HAVE POWER. REMIND YOURSELF TO PRACTICE THESE FOUR THINGS EVERY DAY.

I will practice keeping my thoughts positive each and every day.

1. Start each day with My Special Reminder:
   I will say:

_____

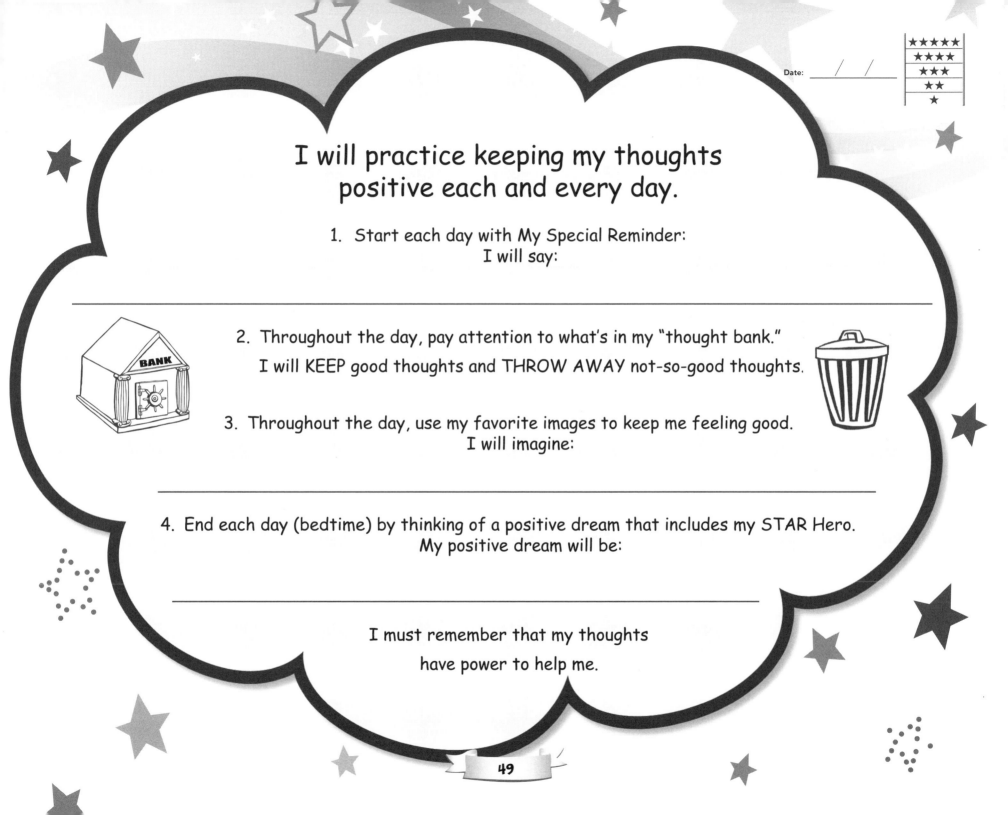

2. Throughout the day, pay attention to what's in my "thought bank."

   I will KEEP good thoughts and THROW AWAY not-so-good thoughts.

3. Throughout the day, use my favorite images to keep me feeling good.
   I will imagine:

_____

4. End each day (bedtime) by thinking of a positive dream that includes my STAR Hero.
   My positive dream will be:

_____

I must remember that my thoughts

have power to help me.

15

When My STAR Hero Comes Home!

Everyone in your family has had to make many changes while your STAR Hero has been away. Aren't you proud of yourself for growing with these changes? Even when your STAR Hero comes home, life will continue to change.

Let's think about when your STAR Hero returns. You can show how much you love and appreciate your STAR Hero by doing special things. For example, make a welcome-home poster, or talk about the activities on your calendar, or set aside a special time to share this book with your STAR Hero.

On the next page, draw a picture of what you imagine doing with your STAR Hero when your STAR Hero comes home. I know you will think of something fun to do. We all look forward to the time when our STAR Hero comes home.

- -

I have really enjoyed learning about you and your STAR Hero. Thank you for sharing your time with me. Always remember that you have the power to choose to be happy! Choose positive thoughts, feel good feelings, and do great things, even while you STAR Hero is away!

Remember:

- Choose your level for today on the Feelings Ladder and circle it on the next page.
- Record your level for today with an X on the Feelings Check-In Graph (appendix).
- Choose one thing to do to stay in touch with your STAR Hero this week.

- Write it here_____

Enjoy the Moment!

Date: ____/____/____

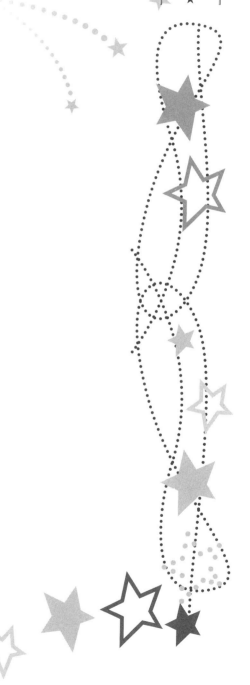

Appendix

Feelings Check-In Graph

Great! ★★★★★															
Pretty Good! ★★★★															
Okay. ★★★															
Not So Good. ★★															
Pretty Bad. ★															
Activity #	1	2	3	4	5	6	7	8	9	10	11	12	13	14	15

Feeling Words

Happy	EXCITED	Sad	Proud	Grumpy
Mad	Frustrated	Guilty	Confident	Embarrassed
Worried	**Scared**	SURPRISED	Joyful	Nervous

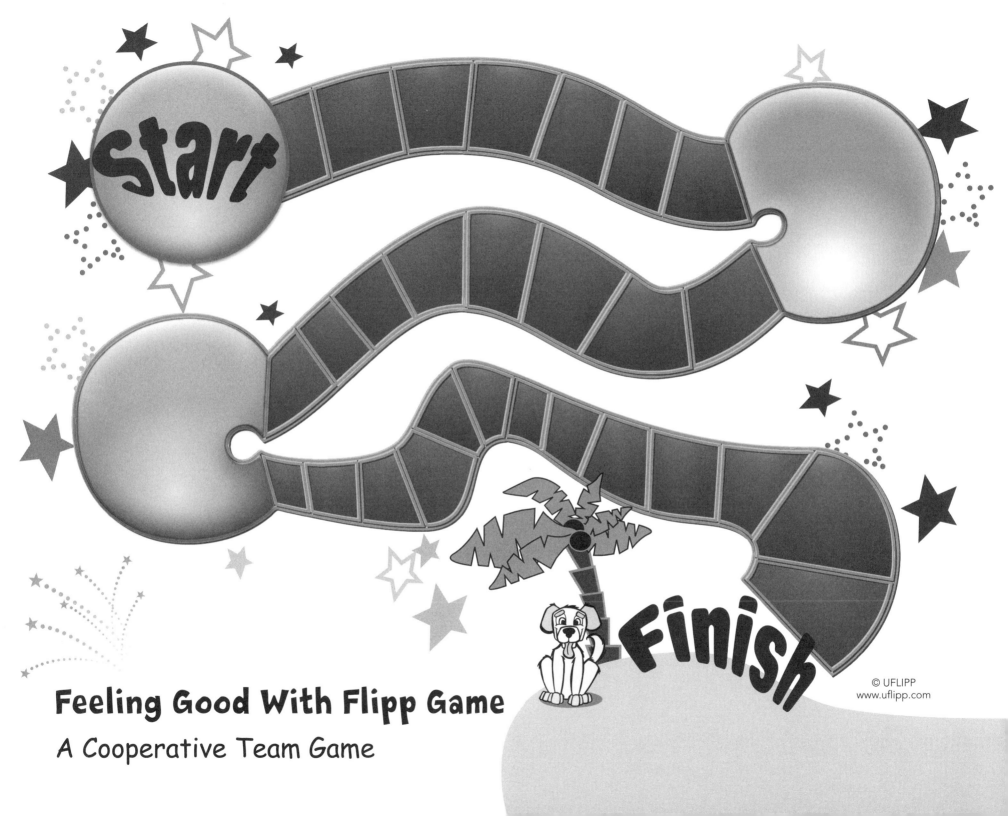

Feeling Good With Flipp Game

A Cooperative Team Game

Feeling Good With Flipp Game Cards

A Cooperative Team Game

I chose to go to bed on time. Go forward 3 spaces. 	I chose to eat a healthy snack. Go forward 3 spaces. 	I chose to ride my bike. Go forward 2 spaces. 	I chose to help at home. Go forward 2 spaces. 	I chose to take a walk. Go forward 3 spaces.
I chose to build a fort. Go forward 2 spaces. 	I chose to feed my pet. Go forward 2 spaces. 	I chose to create art. Go forward 2 spaces. 	I chose to get my homework done. Go forward 3 spaces. 	I chose to play outside. Go forward 2 spaces. 
I chose to play with a friend. Go forward 2 spaces. 	I chose to feel proud of my STAR Hero. Go forward 3 spaces. 	I chose to stay up really late. Go back 1 space. 	I chose to play video games too long. Go back 1 space. 	I chose to tell a lie. Go back 1 space.

Feeling Good With Flipp Game Cards

A Cooperative Team Game

 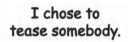

I chose to tease somebody. Go back 1 space. 	I chose to watch too much TV. Go back 1 space. 	I chose to eat junk food. Go back 1 space. 	I chose Not to do my homework. Go back 1 space. 	I chose to fight with my brother or sister. Go back 1 space. 
I chose to talk back to my parent. Go back 1 space. 	I chose to take a bath or shower. Go forward 3 spaces. 	I chose to brush my teeth twice today. Go forward 3 spaces. 	I chose Not to take a bath or shower. Go back 1 space. 	I chose Not to brush my teeth. Go back 1 space.
I chose to share my snack. Go forward 2 spaces. 	I chose to ask for help. Go forward 3 spaces. 	I chose to be respectful to others. Go forward 3 spaces. 	I chose to write a letter to my STAR Hero. Go forward 3 spaces. 	I chose to help others. Go forward 3 spaces.

Thought Bank Bingo Gameboard

B	I	N	G	O
	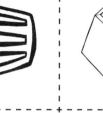	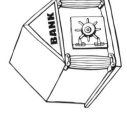		
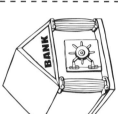		**FREE SPACE**		
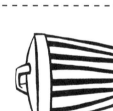			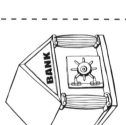	
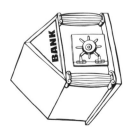	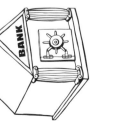			

© UFLIPP
www.uflipp.com

Thought Bank Bingo Game Cards

I hate my friend.	I never get to see my STAR Hero.	I can learn.	I'm horrible at math.	I'm fat.	I keep trying.
I feel alone without my STAR Hero.	I like to play with my pet.	I got a letter from my STAR Hero.	I'm stupid.	I'm healthy.	I'm good.
I think she's mean.	I like myself.	I'm proud of my STAR Hero.	I hate myself.	Somebody loves me.	I don't like school.
I have friends.	I can do it.	That's too hard for me.	I'm bad.	I'm helpful.	I'm afraid I'm not good enough.
No one likes me.	I feel good when I get things done.	I do my work.	I like school.	I can't do anything right.	I like to do something special with family.
I have good memories of my STAR Hero.	I don't have any friends.	People like me.			

Calendar Page

MONTH _____

S	M	T	W	Th	F	S

You have permission to copy this calendar page for each month.